If There Were End Times, They'd Look Like These

Dave Kelly

Spuyten Duyvil
New York City

For Sylvia
(my wife)

IF THERE WERE END TIMES,
THEY'D LOOK LIKE THESE

NIGHT WATCH

On the sea at night you are always alone.
No matter how many others stand about you,
you only need look up to see a star from
which a part of you is looking down. And
in the darkness between you, nothing else
exists. In time, this knowledge enters you
and you will stand forever in a silent darkness.

JANUARY 6, 2021

I don't feel well, you know, it's my stomach.
Maybe it's something l ate or the riots
without apology. Maybe it's the needle at the
executioner's table at the end of a dream.

You could say it was a schooners prow backing
out, leaving a ten-foot hole amid ships and
vanishing in darkness while we search for lifeboats
and they watch on the shore, unsmiling as we sink.

Clutching at driftwood or my brothers, calling
for our help in Morse Code, I don't feel
like a party or falling in love, so accept this
instead, just the wave of a tired wrist and
I'll go on here alone, waiting for nothing…

squatting at the campsite, abandoned by century, a
cannibal in search of his lost anthropologist, he
sifts through ashes to see how cold the breakfast fire,
how far they have run in their little escape because

no one is Catholic anymore, nobody is Baptist, Kosher, or
even owns their own toothbrush. As historians imply:
history is. Meanwhile the infant smiles or feels
gas on its stomach, and sleeps in its trajectory, the
aircraft flying above as soft and loving as a kiss

or the arc of a lullaby. Music speaks unto one side,
reason to the other. Disgusted, the guest leaves.
Tomorrow's divorce will be amicable, even pleasant;
Tomorrow's breakfast will be at the fire on time.

WHAT IS HERE, WHAT IS NOT HERE

She holds a small mirror up to the sun and peers into it
as she lies on the sand, her legs out into the ebbing water
folding over them then draining back into the sea that is
a dark green now, all the way to the horizon. About a hun-
dred yards out, waves come up slightly over a wrecked ship
from an earlier century. It has been looted and is empty
of treasure but not of the dead.

Back in the house beneath me at this window, her husband is
making a door from a slab of half-finished spruce that washed
in last night. It will be a door to the pantry installed
last winter when work had moved inside. Yesterday I found a
shark's tooth on the beach. A couple million years ago a salt
sea covered what are now freshwater lakes and rivers from
Detroit to the Mississippi River.

People will store food in the pantry in this house before it is
covered in water again.

The whine of an electric saw cuts through the afternoon's thick
silence. Gulls accustomed to fresh water rise a few feet in the air
fluff their wings, then settle back into the waves.

ON SHORE

A week after we arrived here something broke
inside me and I spent the summer, first in
Emergency, then Recovery, examination one and
two and then our place here at the Big Lake.

When we were young it was the Big Lake because
you can't see the other shore, but now it is
because we're old and can't run down the dunes
into the waves and swim far beyond our depth.

And now, when they bring me tea instead of
whiskey and ask "How are we doing?" I say "Fine."
and tell them that the Ottawa left their camp
south of here and swam out to save white farmers

working harvest boats in autumn who were dying
in the wreckage of an unexpected storm, among
crops that they had grown and they smile as I tell
them that half the men were lost that afternoon.

THE BOYS

As I understand it, Russian scholars and
young men in the suburbs of Chicago killed
other boys and landladies out of curiosity.
The Russians were often struck down by brain
fever and torn by guilt afterwards and the
Americans went to prison and were knifed by
fellow inmates or sat comforting the others
as they died in epidemics. In all, murder was
useful to others, as is war to our many nations.

Today a group of young boys swim in the lake
outside my window. One of them calls out football
signals as he leaps through the waves; another
calls plaintively to his mother for a towel.
She shouts back for him to "Stay out there!" and
I suspect she is embarrassed by this. As she feels
her husband is a weakling too, she has had a
few men this past summer. Now the little quarterback
dunks her son, then lets him up gasping, crying
now, still calling for his mother, seeking air.

THE CONDEMNED

Having done what I shouldn't, I can lie
on the rug with my dog and dream my own death;
we tremble, our eyes shudder, roll up, then close
again. Having failed to do what I should have
I can listen again to Mother say nice things to my
sister as she pretends I have left the room
forever while I am removed from my name,
from my smile, from the boy of me, from peace.

In the death house the condemned think like that.
They draw their blankets up around their shoulders;
huddled over fires the guards made them put out
they try to sleep, hoping to wake up in the
worst place they have ever been but this one
and when the photographer comes they don't smile.
No one ever eats what they call his last meal.
In the house of the dead they all think like that.

After those deaths, I knew I had been to a place
I would never come back from. I knew I would
never see the same things in my dreams again.
After all of those deaths, I knew I would never
hold my own life as if it were safe in my hand;
I would never share understanding of the word
warm, that voices from life could not speak to me.

In the cells of the condemned they think like that.
Unaware they've slept, they wake to faces of
strangers, staring at them from carved granite;
they shudder, then sigh, then walk among the silent
who have died before them and before whom they die.

GENTLE

In this soft rain my friends are gone
but pleasant in my mind. Even anger
and regret are light memories and as
distant as the sweetest of them in this
quiet air outside my opened window. Leaves
and rain create a pad of distance and I
draw them with a mind that learns to forget.

MOMENT

As I watch a workboat pass between two trees
in the space outside my window, I see the men,
four of them, walking about the deck, tightening
ropes and trading obscenities about the town
they'll spend the night in just ahead. I remember
reading somewhere that sailors once believed that
if they learned to swim they'd doom themselves
to death at sea and wondered if a few were still
believers. It's been raining for two days now, a
soft, gentle rain devoid of joyfulness or sorrow
and life feels quiet, almost pleasant in my mind
as I watch the workboat and its voices drifting out
beyond the shorebound trees into the silent waves.

THE RIGHT THING TO DO

There is a pope at the window.

There is an evangelist at the front door.

There is a killer in the basement:

(I'm going down to the basement.)

POLLY SIGH ONE: MISS LIBERTY SPEAKS

Some people
don't want to die
so they leave their homes
and come to America
where, sometimes,
they have to sleep on railroad bridges.

Early the next morning
they are run over by a train
and several are killed.

The survivors
are arrested by the authorities
and sent back to their homes
with the bodies of their relatives and friends.
There
they are met by the authorities

and taken out
and killed.

POLLY SIGH TWO: SHE SPEAKS AGAIN

Go back!

ONE RAINY DAY

I hate to say the waves are "crashing in"
upon the rocks below, but that's the best way
to describe them. I look for words that surprise
but sometimes the cliche is best. Conversely,
unexpected words excite but have no place to go,
as when I woke from this morning's nap with"sang
froid" on my mind. Thrilled, I rose up from my
sheets and sped to my desk. At the Smith-Corona
(CLASSIC 12) I discovered I didn't know what
these words meant. The choices now were: do I
use them anyway or look them up and let them have
their proper usage? O.K. I decide to move ahead
the way that you might use a whore without knowing
who she is or where she's from, then, done with her
and calmly, slightly, ask about her meaning.

MEANDER

Stalin chose his name because it means
steel in Russian. I read that back in
high school when I looked him up because
I'd drawn him in a death pool we had made
of public figures over sixty. There were
many of them then, all men except for Golda
Mier: Adenaur, Eisenhower, Churchill, De
Gaulle, names were left in the hat when we
had each picked one. Our history teacher
disapproved, but not enough to notify the
principal, and classmates wrote it off as
games the geeks will play. I think of all
this now because I woke up from a dream some
sixty-five years later with the word "steel"
or "steal" and wonder what I had been thinking.

IF THERE'S A GOD, IT LACKS PITY

Today I hate any use of the phrase
"as good as new." I've been lying here
and no part of my body fits it. I watch
a lady bug crawl slowly up the window
screen beside me. I told her that her
house is on fire; she ignored me. Her kids
must all be dead now. I hit her with
a fly swatter earlier this morning. She
fell, but was back there when I woke up
from my nap. I decided to let her live out
her days naturally. I'm 83. They bite, you know.

RACHEL

I just got a call from Rachel at Dealer
Services. It looks to her like my coverage
has expired. If I want to discuss this, I
can press one. Press one what? I wonder. I
ask her, but she just tells me to press nine.
This will end these calls. Now I have ten of them
to press and I still don't even know just what
they are. For a minute I hate Rachel. I was
asleep when she called and this isn't even my
phone; it's Sylvia's. But a pretty boat goes
by outside and I was born into a Christian
family, so I forgive her and go back to my nap.

MATURITY

"I wept because I had no Guccis
until I met a man who had no Florsheims."
                    (Mike Royko)

Sometimes everything goes wrong:
the car won't start, the toilet backs up, God is dead,
the toast is burnt. Sometimes your lawyer has
nothing to say in your defense, the album
is mysteriously empty at the page that showed
a picture of the trophy you told everybody you had won;
sometimes, just before they throw the switch
you forget the little prayer the chaplain gave you.

Well, today it's about forty when it was
supposed to be about eighty-five and arthritis
is killing me and my dog sees another dog
he wants to meet and breaks another leash. . .
STOP! You are saying all of this because
you did a lousy job on the new siding
and now the wall leaks in the rain. Breathe easy; look
at me; now, say this: "Okay. I did it. Yes,
it is all my fault. I'm sorry. I'll fix it."
There. That's better. Now just shut up.

THE MONARCHS

A small flight of butterflies is working
in the tree outside my room this afternoon. My
first thought is how pleased Sylvia will be
they have come back this summer, then of
flagpoles in Honolulu, jungles in the heart of
Guatemala, the width of the lake here they
must cross so early on their trip, the long
drive back to our home in New York and the
strangeness of a car that starts up when you
throw a switch that also lights a room and
kills a man convicted of his brother's death.
Then I notice one of them is bright red among
the orange tones of its mates and that it's
long past noon, he's probably been dead since
late last night, and that they killed him
with a needle filled with poison, not a shock.

MIRAJ

Today I tried to write something for

two dead men. My mind seemed to be working
but my fingers, paper, ink all seemed to fail.

I gave up. I jotted something in a note
that was no song or tried to be one. I

folded it, went downstairs, greeted guests
all in a rage, never knowing if I'd failed

or even tried to save them.

The end of this last week brings us
its rain, like veins of glass.

Morning is a long sigh's distance

from the night's final hint of light.

SEX ON THE BEACH

and "It's a drink," somebody says and,
"Why, " I ask, "Does it have sand in it?"
and you say, "That's gross," and I say
"No, what's gross is if you're trying to
feed your kids their peanut/butter/jelly
sandwiches and somebody is having sex on
th…" "Just cut it out!" you say, "Why
are you always being such an asshole?"
and I reply, "that's better than being the
idiot who thought up sex on the beach,"
and you say, "Idiot is not allowed anymore."

MAKE SOMEONE HAPPY

Guests always ask for what they ate
the last time they were here and it's
the first time they've had it in a year
or two, but we have lots of guests, so
I'm staring at the eighteenth plate of
clam spaghetti that I've had since early
June. Which is why a CD of Dinah Washing-
ton on "Love for Sale" lies this morning
under a dozen slogan T-shirts in a drawer
upstairs, even though I've played it every
morning since I bought it last November.
And Horace Silver's 1959 recording of
"Senor Blues" rests on the table beside
the cookbook I've left open to "Spare Ribs."

AMERICA!

Imagine that; Corn ground up, then toasted
into crisp and tasty squares, then poured
into a bowl with milk and crunchy sugar for
my pleasure, before I must go anywhere at all!

THE HOLIDAYS

Red flags are up today, warning swimmers
to stay back on shore. A record sum of
drownings has plagued The Lakes this year
but a virus has claimed more, and mad men
roam towns and highways, shooting strangers,
so exact numbers have become as unimportant
as metaphors for God at the grave sites of
the poor. Still, when the waters calm, the
boats come out and people laugh among the
waves and deaths have never happened here.

THE TYPING LESSON

I got to the end of the fourteenth line of
what I was just writing before I looked up
at the thirteenth and saw I had made a mistake.
It was a whole wrong word, not just a typo, so
I couldn't mend it with a strikeover, so I
quit and now here I am. I can't go back, delete,
and correct, because this isn't a computer,
which my wife says I should buy. This is an
old, mechanical/portable typewriter (Smith-Corona
Classic 12) just like the one I got for graduation
fifty-seven years ago and I am tortured and
stubborn, as with many of my choices. My lady
has gone into town to come back with treasures.
Today she'll buy a coffee maker because the
one she purchased yesterday won't work and
must be replaced, like everything that doesn't
work until it's a replacement and no one does
the work you paid them for first time it's done.
This has become a new third world country;
even its President is being patched and
made over by his latest replacement and even he
threatens to return and do his own repairs.
We are staying at a summer home on a Lake
geographers call "Great." It's too large to
be called a "darling little cottage," but
and here I stop: two lines ago I replaced "small"
with "large," the word I had intended. Now
I've fixed it. I feel complete. Now I shall stop.

VIEW

In another country, boys return home
carrying their rifles, intent on killing
their fathers, already murdered. Somewhere
else, a mother slices off a piece of onion
and folds it in dark bread. She gives it
to her oldest son to give him strength to
hunt for meat to feed the rest. At the shore
waves slide back from shore, revealing the
bones of a schooner sunk there a hundred
years ago. Today three dark spars as long
as trees spread from the wreck into the sea.

TRIBES

The casino here belongs to people
calling themselves the Little River Band
of Odawah, or Ottawa we called our high
school when I was young, located in Ottawa
Hills in our town and in Toledo to the
east of Detroit and in Ohio. A dictionary
on my desk refers them to the Ojibwa or
Ojibway, names heard more widely through
the state of Michigan, or Potowatamy, a
name I heard often through my youth.
They say no virgin timber grows across
this state, stripped of it by a man named
Lansing and some others whose names appear
on all our maps. Our capitol bears his name
and his trees, a hundred or so years old
grow in replaced woods. And we've wiped out
the wolverine, and coyote have replaced
the timber wolf and bears have travelled
down from further north. And small white
tribes have gone insane and armed them-
selves and threaten death to everyone they see.

PASTICHE

Handball racketball paddle ball, tennis. Some
are hard and some are for the pleasure. They play
skateboard at the Olympics this summer, with terms
for moves that you can imitate on your computer.
Outside my window two boys are paddling by on things
shaped like surfboards, one boy kneeling, one boy
standing; the upright boy is leading, if this is
a race. I haven't been in water in four years
now and don't expect I will be until they pour me
from a box. I wonder if the lake will recognize
me, perhaps return the gold ring I lost swimming
in one summer rain. Today I wear glasses to take off
to watch the scenes outside my window and put back
on to tell you what it is that I have seen.

IF THERE WERE END TIMES, THEY'D LOOK LIKE THESE

I have lost track of my notes
while saying a desperate rosary
to my twin for the health of
the ailing president. In the
desert, a miraj is a waking dream.
It is not always of water or
even respite from suffering. We
came to Jerusalem hoping to be
told everything would be better.
Now the stars are dying one by one
above the landmarks we put under
them, the gods laugh bitterly
behind the portraits we invented.

HOSPICE

Every year the Monarchs come here on their
way to Guatemala and I wonder if they know
they aren't the ones who'll make it there.
Never mind, though, they go on sucking the
juices from the tree on our hill, resting
among its leaves, building the strength to
put their offspring on the west shore of the
giant lake that they'll die crossing. Some
years they've been a metaphor as I watched
them and my own children drifting through the
August light and other summers I have watched
this woman see to the fallen and the broken
as they paused in their flights to future.

HOW MANY FACES DO YOU SEE IN THIS PICTURE?

At his desk in a small, two-man office, an accountant stops works and looks up at the blue wall before him. He thinks of his ex-wife. He sees her standing at a bus stop with a friend, another woman. As they speak, his wife tugs with her right hand at a lock of hair over her left eye, a gesture he has never seen her use. In upstate New York, it is January and the temperature is approaching zero.

On Galveston Island, a house on the bay side has five months before a hurricane tears it apart.

Just five minutes before they go to their bus, a group of math students in a Jesuit school in Nogales, Arizona, are given the sentence, "This statement is false." to analyze at home that night.

There are the faces of three children at the front window of the house on Galveston Bay.

ANOTHER SHORT HAPPY LIFE

The new kitten thinks her name is Godammit!
I understand; that was my name at a certain
age. These days it's What's the matter now? and
my wife and I use it for each other several
times a day. But these things change, unless you
are the child removed from possibility or the
boy whose death in a small war was decided by
a bicycle accident at ten. The calculus of all
our lives is filled with error; the blame is no
one's. Meanwhile, the little cat decides to learn
what lives across the highway. Again: God Damn It!

HIM

His footsteps tap the concrete walk;

a house dog shudders in its sleep.

He turns his collar up against a chill;

his head turns down to watch the path before him.

When he walks along these empty streets each night

even the blind draw window shades against him.

ANOTHER T-SHIRT

It says:

> "SARCASM

it's what I do best" on the front and I don't recall
which daughter gave it to me, but it means something different
whichever one it's from. I put it in a drawer I almost never
go into, but today I almost fell down in the shower, so
I need a new and stronger sense of my identity. I think of
Gary Spees in college and John McElwee back in high school,
whose bigotry was the only sense of self they had, and
of my mother whose disdain for my father and his kin gave her
the power in our house. Today I'm eighty-three and need some
grab bars in the bathroom and a cane and bannister on
flights of stairs. Still, when I fall down, I need somebody's
help to get back up. But I know who I am. The T-shirt goes back.

DETROIT SONNET

Our new car is the best car in the world.
Our new car will start itself, steer itself,
go to the store, shop for you and you won't
have to tell it or the boys in Japan that
is just what you want in the whole damn world.

But back home, the new car misses payments; it
will bankrupt your whole family, call its own
repo man who'll take your job and crush your
lunch pail as it drives away. Then, you can
live in its shelves in the garage and warm

yourself in your old blue shirt, read union cards
and retirement plans as your sweet wife drives
by in her new chauffeur's cap in a brand new best
car with a fat salesman in back making phone calls.

MOB

First you kill because you wanted to
and then you make up reasons for it.
The chants and names you shouted only
meant to bring you here, and not that
you meant them. And what you had, that
tomorrow you'll say was a reason was just
this twisting whirl of darkness you loved
before you locked your arms with others
and threw your mind aside and jumped into.

HONOR

The men these streets were named for
have never walked here. Still, we die
each time we're called to add a few
more streets to lie beneath their names.

ACHILLES

They keep me here in the daylight.
At night they bring me out again to play.
I'm fitted in the costumes of the wars
they've learned to love that history
would rather they had learned to put away.

When they come marching, the downbeat in
each pair of steps falls on the wrong foot
and their eyes, when turning right, don't see
that they are looking out, not looking in
where the evil they pretend to fight will be

when their battle had been won and blood
and smoke mix in the cup to invented gods
and artificial heroes and to artificial
truths no one left alive can feel at all.

HOW ARE YOU TODAY, DAVE?

Something is leaching the color from
my left arm. It's been half a year since
I allowed myself a full meal and I still
could lose about a hundred pounds and
not look thin; even with a cane, I walk
like a giant toddler with an intense fear
of falling, and half my teeth and hair
have disappeared. I won't show you the stuff
growing on my toenails, thanks. And you?

THE KILLER

He turns his collar up against the chill,

his head down to watch his path before him;

his footsteps tap against the concrete walk.

When he walks these streets at night,

The house dogs shudder as he passes through
their sleep, and

even the blind have drawn down their shades.

DARKNESS

A parent wakes from the dream of a child dying.

CASE Q# 107 TELEVISION ADDICT

He died, of course, but there he was each Saturday
after five days of guest hosts, looking a little tired
but still knowing all the answers written on his little
cards and making sure that even the dummies who didn't
get to stay on 'till the end felt good about themselves.
I always knew one or two of the answers, so I watched
every night, sometimes getting three on Saturdays, and
marvelling at the changes in his hair from week to week.

Five Rants Against High School History

Ending In A Ballad For Jessie James

WAKE UP

Outside my window somebody's radio sings
in the tasered voice of a cartoon rabbit
that we should what sounds like kick an
unnamed person called "him" in the ass like
our Uncle Charley. Perhaps I've been sleeping
too long, perhaps not long enough. When another,
this time a female in a bubble machine tells
me to throw off my ventilator and kill the
President, I vow to leave the journalists alone
if or when I am awake. And now a chilled wind
follows this lack of music into the room
and my eyes are open and not filled with snow.
Okay, it's Tuesday, late morning, early after-
noon and I'm right here: chilled a little,
half alert, not ready for the guests we had
last Friday. It's late in the first quarter
of a century and we've all been driven a
little more than mad by plagues and mad men
to the point where we've lost our syntax,
grammar, and twelfth grade vocabulary, all
the language tools we thought we'd need, all
the "language tools" to make a bad dream end.

AWAKE 2

Today, at its center, looks like
the present moment. I must assume
from this that I have no plans for
the rest of it and have been at this
point since early morning. You may,
of course, suggest that I must have
come here at some time from another
place, since I am not dressed as I
normally am when I sleep, so I must
have made certain decisions that
have brought me here. I am unable
to respond to this, however, since
this is as I wrote it and conditions
cannot be changed. You, however, can
reply that, since you have this in
your hand and read it at a time I
do not inhabit, there has been a change
of our conditions. I must respond
though, since I am still here writing,
we must still exist at this place in
its writing and there has been no
change here upon which you can comment.

2021

Reservation:

Party of Lincoln?

Table for none.

THE BALLAD OF JESSE JAMES

When I was a boy, the movies said that
Jesse was a hero, that rode against the
barons who had stolen his home and killed
his Mother. Yes, she was a capital M, and loved
her white boys and the little colored lad whose
parents succumbed to disease somewhere. And Monday,
back in school, they never mentioned Quantrell
or his Raiders or that Frank & Jesse rode with
him, they didn't compromise and spilled lots of
blood in Kansas and Missouri and deserved the
rope they didn't get. School and movies also didn't
say that The Kid in old New Mexico was fined
for littering each time he shot a Navajo or that
way back East there were these folks old Andy
Jackson made to walk a couple thousand tears
before we let them live a little north.

BOARD GAMES

Failure, success, the Vampire Game:
who gets to interview the Art King and who
will smuggle the camera into the death house?

Now the children kneel around the table,
its legs cut down for play, and roll
the big dice: aces and eights, a passed game,
green hills for the lame, Picassos for the blind;
growing up in America is like growing up,

in America. If I smoke the Camels, who
lives in the blue house? Who owns the lone wolf?

And who goes home with the empty food tray
or calls the electrician, never home?

Every morning I open the office, just
a candy salesman with a few from The Times,
a few words of madness, jokes about bowel gas;

every night I go home to the cold glass and
its pipe, to the cat and her bird-let it go,
that twenty-year-old thing of dead feather,
its mate calling for help at the window, its
song one thin dime, its one wing two quarters.

In the playroom the calm make fun of the dying;
in the ice house the tongue waits for the lemon;
the bison, nobody's coat, cries from thirst
among apostrophes and geometric cubes. So,

the parahelpers tell us, if you want to be
mad you can be serious, otherwise look out
for that self you have left: it's only one

and you can see almost at once, it's dangerous.

THE ROCKS BELOW

The waves were ruthless that night as
they crashed on the rocks below. He stirred
the smaller pieces of wood to make the fire
burn more broadly. It was juniper in the
dry gin that always made him strange, he
thought, but vowed he wouldn't kill anyone
just the same. Still, when he looked into the
bathroom mirror that morning, there were traces
of blood on his cheekbones and at the corner
of his mouth. Oh mercy me, he mused, have
I gone astray again? He tried to turn the light
switch of his darkened memory, but nothing
showed itself there. He would ask the guard
who stood outside his room each night, but
the detail were sworn to silence about
anything they witnessed in the residence.
He was protected until he left office, from
himself as well as those who had elected him.

POOR MAN'S PRAYER

Our Father which art in heaven, hallowed be thy bread,
thy hand, my mouth hallowed by my knees, this road in
the raining turning slowly into ice, and blessed be the
house that turns its back to me, light shining in on itself.

Carelessly then, we see they will always be with us and
with the slow craft of the architect we build their homes,
one by the sea for the rain and one in the desert, to
make the most of the sun only we can own, only those of
the table, laughing at the voices of men in black robes.

Ghost of night sleepers, of pressed crease and closed road,
a guard stands at the end, smiling with his selection.

On the last day then, dust for the soup, stones for the
bowl, that day and these are our children and the others;
there are the ones without tears, without a pin to count
on, arguing as they diminish, separated mind and body

deprived of themselves, philologists waiting at dawn
for the check, watching the Postman as they have learned
as he turns away and walks down some other street.

THE REVOLUTION AS TELEVISED THIS YEAR

As I understand it, Santa Anna killed John Wayne
at the Alamo for stealing Texas and Billy the Kid
was fined for littering each time he shot a Yaqui
down in New Mexico way. The great states of Hollywood
and Texas have plenty more to say each time a new
history book rolls off the presses (ask Johnny
Appleseed about the dying chestnut trees) or Honest
Abe gives new birth to the Mississippi dead. This
morning, patriots are marching on our highways where
you leave I-80 for I-94, from Detroit to Colorado, or
into a state house where a governor waits for the
madmen to come and take her life. Jesus weeps in the
temples of the poor and thunders oaths and threats
of death in the "houses of worship" where white
organists play Bach and choirs chant a battle cry
of freedom from the peaceful, glory to death's god.

CAPTAIN JACK ON THE GALLOWS

They stuffed dirty rags against the death song
in his mouth and chained his legs together so
he couldn't dance. But he died anyway, and not
the way they thought he would, and now the trail
in Oregon is not a place a white man wants to die.

WASHING AMERICA

Ahh, there! Maybe a shower and a shave will
scrub me cleaner then the walls of Congress,
betrayed out of Lincoln's name by the proud
ignorant, mocked by treason and disgrace. An
eagle passes by my bedroom window out to sea
and, if he were real, I'd wonder if he would
ever fly this way again. We are surrounded by
oceans covered with a film of waste; a match
would sear the cover off and leave remorse.
Perhaps a bath of roses and gardenias will be
just the thing to bring fresh odors to us and
our Capitol, perhaps a lemon scrub will let
us walk out to fresh air and inhale again.

THE DREAM EDITOR

In his mind they were singing Irish
folk songs and the dancers kept on
clattering on hard wooden floors and
the smell of fresh lamb roasting over
charcoal filled the remotest corners
of the little house. But it wasn't so,
you understand, it was a spider bit him
on the neck while he was sleeping in
the night. When he woke there'd be a
lump that hurt when he touched it and
itched when he did not and the jailer
would be standing at the cell door with
a glass of brandy in his right hand and
a rope tied in a noose held in the left.
But that wasn't the truth either, as he
came up through the fog a second time,
knowing brandy is not allowed in the
prisons of his country, and they'd wake
him thoroughly so he could watch the
long procedure, so he went on sleeping
as the music turned to drum rolls and
the trumpet calls of Spanish death and
the wooden floors to clouds in his mind.

JOE AND ADOLPH IN ANOTHER WORLD

After we called her by your first wife's name
I wondered if we would ever see you again and
when you didn't make that call at Christmas, I
knew we weren't friends anymore. I am sorry for
the dogs tho, both Alsatians with good papers,
goodness! what fine puppies they'd have made, and
I would just have wanted the pick of the litter and
you could have taken all the rest, and little
Mimsy would have made a pictured story book about
them that Disney artists might turn into cartoon
delights we'd give ours and our sweethearts' names
to and the world would celebrate us differently.

AT THE FOOT OF THE SCAFFOLD

They all went mad, of course, but only for a couple minutes.

POWER FAILURE

If another storm hits will the lights come on
or am I slipping into magical thinking again? I see
darkness forming at the horizon and the wind is colder
and the pressure is low or high, whatever pressure is
supposed to be when the weather is bad again and the
power's still out from last night's storm. Down the road

a workman falls from his ladder onto a power line and we
wonder if the cable's out or can we sit here, watching
television in the dark? Well no, stupid, media needs
power too, not just chocolate, crackers, marshmallows
and memory. Downstairs someone steps on the cat and she
cries out the way she does a few times every day and I
look back across evil that takes hold even when the
sun is brilliant and memory slips away like liquid gold.

TRYING TO SLEEP WITHOUT GOODNIGHT

The key in what lock, what doorknob turning?
The radio, soft down the hall, cat leaping
on the night's back, just for the ride, just so
those eyes as we slip downward. . . cookies, yes
cookies, perhaps, and the whole cup of something
warm, the pillow fat and chilled right. I wait
for the bitterness to replace memory then be
forgotten, the face behind the mirror, the empty
cupboard, the gaunt dog, the bowl with its spoon
dry and the unforgiving children, father, the mother
with nothing more to do, everyone awake, yet,
when you go to bed hungry you go there alone.

MEMORY

The week begins with the door left open,
with the book turned to a page with your
name on it, with a smile and a sigh, how
you could fight in your prime, how you
left the ring with your hair unmussed and
the knowledge that your door was open to

thieves. The week begins on a day, the day
on a page, its name underlined, not the son
of champions, but someone whose name we forget
easily, unmarked on any page but this, unknown
by a self, untouched by words that can't be spoken.

THE WORD

For years you heard it in the back of
your head: is this the end of it? the last
thing happening? am I ending or is it
all of it. . . but now it's in the forefront
every morning no, it has never been this hot
this far north, the water reaches to this
height along this shore, the people of
this land have never killed in such great
numbers and with a rage so all-consuming!

We have lived in the hills, at the center of
a valley, and on flat plains of grass you
could fatten cattle on, always with a window
on the long view. We were aware of clouds,
aware of the fires moving in from the West,
the ice from the North. Teaching the child
to spell its own name, we are aware that,
unless you learn to write it properly, you
will return to the grave; no one will save you.

For years you have heard it daily: the week
begins with a day, the day with a name, unknown
by self, untouched by words we never can speak.

AND FELL TO HIS DEATH ON THE ROCKS BELOW

I've run this line through my head more
than a thousand times since we got here
and I looked down from my window at the
ruined beach and the giant stones they've
poured at the shoreline to save our hill.
So far I've reached the thoughts that you'd
need a greater height to die on a mound of
sand and that a Middle Eastern parking lot
must look much like this after we've bombed
it. Right now I'm watching my grandson on
the last step on our stairway, deciding not
to swim, and my daughter at the top of the
hill watching, and thinking of the many times
I must have disappointed my own mother and
how I might have saved my life each time I
did. I was a fortunate child, having never
been threatened by unruly parking lots or Ameri-
can bombs and having struggled only at play
with Syrian friends to push each other off
a diving raft in the middle of Long Point Lake.
Still, I feel we're falling to the rocks below.

CHAPTERS

The older generation sits on the shore
while the younger one swims. Then a younger
one will join them. The oldest enjoys the
cool air and the sound of voices. Some days
there is less of this; there is never any more.

THE FALL OF KABUL

Kabul is falling in color.
I can't remember if Saigon fell in black and white
or not, but the Chosin Reservoir went down
on the radio and Paris fell with Bogart in Paris.
Still, even at my age the losses our
bleak minds create for what we like to call our Mother
leave a hollow in the hands and wrists
and a tired ache between my shoulders that seem
shameful when I realize what pain waits
at this place we're watching, we're
discussing over Sunday's coffee, rolls and milk.
Right now I'm thinking of a phone call
from a colleague who had worn a rifle and had
been a student and had been a teacher
and was watching as part of Asia
slipped our grasp and a letter
I am writing to a colleague
who had taught me as I taught her
and who looks now at a son
as I look now at my own daughters' children
with diminished hope for this place
we still sometimes call our Mother.

REQUIEM

When he was dying, he asked that he be buried
in a place where small children played, perhaps
as ashes mixed in the sand they poured into
their pails with little shovels, and their laugh-
ter would pour like ripples through the rocks in
a cool stream through the days he disappeared
into. When he said this a large dog, dark and
very old, lay sleeping at his feet, and when he
had finished speaking, they both were silent
there for what seemed to be an endless time.

THE ALLIANCE

My dreams of becoming
a five-star general or
heavyweight champion of

the world have not
come true so I con-

sole myself with this
ham and cheese sandwich.

On the other hand you
went to a better college
and I am smarter than

you which we both know

so I cut the sandwich in
two and we share it. Then

you sleep with my wife
and I kill your dog in the
driveway coming home. Our

neighbor says that we must
talk, so we kill him and
share another sandwich.

THE DEALER

Seven of these?

Yes, seven

Seven of these?

Yes, Seven

Seven?

Seven.

Sev. . .

No. Six.

WHY I DIDN'T VOLUNTEER

One day I pretended I only had

one arm.

And it wasn't pleasant.

KABUL, THIS TIME

I have read the Koran and not found why
the sound of gentle waves falling on sand
like this should make a man kill children
for their laughter and I have looked into
the testaments of Christians and of Jews
for explanations of bombs falling on small
villages and making flames of ripe fruits
and golden sheaves of wheat from a sky as
clear as this. But even the sweetest child
fails to roll back the fires that consume
a world we once thought we were perfecting
on our hopes. The jealous gods and hating
gods these pages speak of have prevailed,
their stories tell us only of despair.

THE COMEDIAN

If he fails to laugh at these thoughts
in his mind, he must weep at them forever.

CALCULUS

A wasp has entered here. He dances
among the children. They are frightened,
the older ones quietly, the younger
squealing and crying out with less sense
of themselves. The insect passes through them
and shelters among stones in a small
pail brought up from the beach. The girls
quiet, forget the wasp and follow each other
down the hill and into the water. He dozes,
warmed by the sun in his new home. The
air will cool as the afternoon moves on. In
the same way, a dog will come to the bucket,
look inside, perhaps just move along. Others will
come by here; some may pause at this spot,
others will walk past. Eventually, the girls
will return from the lake and up the hill.
Somewhere else a new war is beginning or
a man is raising his hammer to replace a board.

RETIREMENT LETTER

I watch him from my window as he
wraps himself in bug spray with such
care: his neck and arms, his legs
and groin, his clothing, then his
face and hands (his face with these)
and then I notice the fresh shirt and
walking shorts. And later I look upon
myself in the mirror and wonder: how
have you lived to this age, you sloppy
man? Your scraggy beard and uncut hair
(trimmed on occasion with a pair of
kitchen shears), your unplanned lunges
to the right and left as you meandered
here and there. Your rhymes are never
planned and go unnoticed as a rule
and when you get people laughing, it's
because you're such an idiot. And as
I look into myself in the glass, I
think of others I know who write "Author"
in the questionnaire at the spot where
I write "poet" as my profession and
at the office where I vanish in thin air.

THE SIXTEEN LINES IN MY TRASH

This morning I watched the news
then went upstairs to write a poem

on Evil.

KILLING

Saturday mornings my friend Lanny's mother would tie
a chicken upside down by its legs from a clothesline in
her backyard. We would watch from our swings as she hefted
a butcher knife in her right hand and sliced off its head.
Then we'd pick up long sticks and poke at the head on the
ground and, briefly, the beak would snap at our sticks.

Once the headless body slipped its rope and danced in the
dirt, then crumbled. Years later I knew what cliche I'd
just heard meant.

Lanny's mother, Jean, was married to a plumber named Walter.
Everybody called him Hap. We didn't own a car and Hap rented
our garage for his truck and tools and metal pipes. Pipe
was not made of plastic then, although we didn't know this
because it wasn't.

Once I looked in to the back of Hap's panel truck and saw
the dead body of one of his hunting dogs.

The dogs lived in a pen and did not have names and we were
not allowed to play with them. I had a springer spaniel
named Corky and he wouldn't go with me to Lanny's to play.

In the summer, the factories would lay my dad off and Hap
would take him on his truck and they would work all day
and some Saturdays Jean would kill two chickens and my mom
and I would walk down the alley for Sunday dinner and when
we got back home, my dad would be there, drunk.

REJECTION LETTER

I don't feel well today. Maybe I'm sick or ill
(is there a difference?), or maybe I've just worn
myself watching the children playing with the new
kitten in the hot afternoons. I remember hearing
people say of men my age, "That was when he started
going down hill." I miss the hill. There was always
a nice breeze at the top of it and when that wasn't
enough, you could always go down and plunge into the
lake for proper cooling off. This morning I lay
awake and listed people in my head I might go to and
ask for a kidney or a bit of liver; they were all
much younger. It would be a waste to spend a piece
of their health on a carcass like this. Besides,
that same list holds many of the same ones I have
realized I don't wish to outlive. Add ineligible
donors and pets and you'll understand the reason
this list goes into a drawer for no consideration.

"WE ALL WANT TO BE ROCK STARS"
(Rachel Hall)

God, I'm getting so old I'm beginning to stink.
I forgot the date on a change of address and now I owe
fortunes; the IRS wants me; they can't read my scrawl
and I've filled in all the wrong blanks. I can't see
in the photo if it's my mother or a homicidal nun;
yesterday I began weeping loudly at the homeless
as they slept in the shelter in my tv set. . .help me,
take me somewhere for my own good. I'm dreaming about
the war again (I was Cap'n Davey and my wagon and my
bedroom were both painted battleship gray). Alright,
I'll confess: I'm somewhere before Elvis gets
drafted, I hated Ricky Nelson, Pat Boone made me sick,
Okay? There were three persons I wanted to be: Miles
Davis, Humphrey Bogart, and was it Adlai Stevenson
or my cousin Ronny? Well, they're all gone now.

THE SOLOIST

Out on the water a young boy
is raising a sail on his small
boat, alone for the first time.
He is proud, but a little afraid
as he works. Suddenly, the Lake
is entire. No voices correct or
reassure him. And while he is
proud, in time he will regret it.

THE NIGHT DISPATCHER

A man looks out, responsible for the telegraph each night
and for the messages that certain boats will not come home.
In the hours after midnight he sucks on tablets; mornings
he will pace from room to room, drinking occasionally from
a bottle of white liquid for his stomach. He will not die
old. He will watch the young sisters in each other's arms as

they leap from the flames into the waves, the captain return
to the inner cabin to die with his wife, and the deck hand
crawl up the beach, at least a child in his jacket still alive.

He will call the widows and notice nothing like his God hovers
over the nights of snow and darkness that we die in, and
each of his daughters will hate him for telling them this
and for drinking himself and his sorrow into sleep each of those
days they might have walked together dressed for Sunday through

bright streets, beside the docks, and past that water he will not
see, will not look at in the daylight, will not know is there.

THE LAST BUILDER

90 degrees. A mist steams up from the surface
of the lake and drifts in over us. My nurse rolls
soaked towels flat across my body-at first she
had to take care they were not too cold-now the
water from the ground is nearly as warm as my sweat.
I am the only patient left here. Once there were
many of us- the men who brought the smoke and oil
and steel in loud explosions into the clearings
we had thought to live in with great pleasure. Now
I wait as flames come down to meet this earth's
mounting heat and wish this one who comforts me as
I join with dead comrades, safe passage to the comfort
of a land I will not tell her I know will not exist.

WORLD WAR II

I was five. It was my first war.
The radio said we could win if we planted
a garden in our backyard, a Victory Garden.
We had no grass in our backyard. My father
said my dog I would dig it all up
playing and get stains that don't
wash out like dirt does. One morning

he said we'd have to give up my left field
and we left the dog inside and went
out back and dug small holes we put sticks in
and my father pulled mine up and put them
in a straight line like his and tied string
in a straight line of sticks and put
seeds in the holes. Then he tamped dirt down

into each hole and I followed him inside.
My mother sat inside by the kitchen table.
She looked up as we came into the room.
"I planted a Victory Garden," he said.
"For him." and she began crying again.

WOLF HAVEN

A large white stone marks the earth
in the center of young basswood trees
and a leaf falls across its top from
the branches. Perhaps an unfound door

lies under the stone, leading to a place
only of the imagination and I wait with
another to find that place and you.

Educated and cynical, I realize unreality
but, better, the sight of what is not
makes the thought that carries it, because
thought can be repeatable- thus I can

float forever down a cool stream, beneath
flowered branches with you, can drink
from glasses of idea or of laughter and

in the absence of all of this in time will
make it all we need when all we have is now.

JO-LEE

The old man smiles at the woman
he does not remember is his daughter
as she brings iced water to his chair.
She smiles back. She is pretending
to herself that he knows who she is
and thanks her when he says something
she cannot quite make out. Her name
is Jo-Lee. She thinks now she hears
it. This is all right. What he says
as he takes the drink is her name too.

TIME AND SPACE

Every time I turn a corner a whole new world
lies out before me, it's the same routine:
strange faces, measured greetings, the introductions
and challenges, credentials and the knowledge
that, once again, I am an interruption in the lives
of others. It's like going to sleep in New York and
waking up in Chicago: over here the streets are
numbered; over there they all have names. And
when I've finally figured out where I am, it doesn't
matter anymore: the street ends and I have to start again.

BEST IN BREED

I held his head and upper body
in my arms as they shaved his left
rear leg, put in the needle and
pumped the death into him and I
didn't see his dying. What I saw
and it was just before that, was
a moment he was immediately alone.

HE FALLS

He worked a lifetime in the tops
of trees. When he fell from one
to a death below, he might have
wondered quickly as he went, if
he didn't have this dream before.

ASSASSIN

He said that just before they died
they looked up from the knife into
his eyes and said just one word.

"Please."

VIEW

Small bits of clothing in my food or isn't it
the other way around? I'm half-asleep and my mind
can't order senses and perceptions and the words
to use with them. As I'm looking through the win-
dow at a small sail on the horizon, it rises up
to show me that it is a tiny insect wing caught in
the screen, the water is below it and the sky above
and both are farther off than will be imagined by
its owner before it dies. And just a few yards out
stand trees that dwarf this bug I'm watching as
it fights to live and further out the mindless waves
and over all of that the unimaginable spaces of sky.

LABOR DAY 2021

Actually it's Sunday. Labor Day is tomorrow.
The rich will line up to say goodbye to their
boats, the richer 'till they meet again a
month or two from now, and the very rich will
greet other boats they keep for winter pleasures
in another climate, after a hurricane or two.
Up here, I rise up from my morning nap to the
constant knowledge there is much I haven't learned
at 83. Today I don't know if they reverse the
seasons' names south of the Equator, or what the
two words are that I assigned myself to find the
meanings of as I fell asleep two hours ago. But,
as I stumble into the rest of the day, the door
opens and my wife comes in to gather up laundry.
Behind her are a dog named Glee and a young cat
called Whimsey. My wife's name is Sylvia. I am
eighty-three. My memory functions well enough today.

LABOR DAY AGAIN

My neighbor's old school flag flies
just below his Stars and Stripes. I

studied at another school and we trade
friendly insults over this. We compare

old football scores and Nobel winners.
If there had been a revolution on

this day in some past, one of us might
not be flying his flags anymore.

SUMMER IN THE CITY

It's a beautiful morning: cold, no sun, weather in the harbor dark and
forbidding; I slip into a gray shirt and run outside to greet it, breath-
Ing in the industrial-strength smog. A pigeon wheezes, staggering along
the sidewalk beside me, a rusty bicycle leaning against a wall, coughs
retchingly. I hum a popular song of the moment about preachers and
wardens and being lain beneath green green grass at home. As I pass

the house next door, my neighbor silently regards me from his porch
swing, muffled at the throat in a black flannel blanket. Maybe we'll have
gruel for our supper tonight, I muse as I jaunt along, thinking too of
angry nuns, arithmetic and muddied water, maybe I'll watch dogs having
group sex and thrash them with grandma's shillelagh, then we can watch
with popcorn as the newsmen read the night's last death row quotes
and see the politicians waltz like armadillos in the graveyard.

A GENDER DIFFERENCE

At the beginning of the summer
a giant truck tire washed up on the rocks
on our beach. A friend of ours, a man
of fifty, fell in love with it
immediately. It was too large for anyone
to move it out, although he nearly
drowned in trying. One morning waves
had taken it away. He was saddened but lost
interest a few days later. Our wives
and daughters didn't understand
his desire but felt his temporary sorrow.
I understood his need but didn't share
it and I knew the waves erased his loss.

ANALYZING HUMOR AT WHARTON

"That was no lady, that was my wife."

"I don't know, but when he talks, you listen."

"Is a bear Catholic?"

"The poor are always with us."

The firewood on the porch is dwindling away to a precious few
sticks and the oil furnace is on vacation for the decade. As
the subject of the verb, inflames, contemplates his stiff fin-
gers in the waiting room, the dentist watches for the price
of gold to climb a tad bit more while the fools all play at sixes.
Praise God; Pass ammunition; Bless this House O Lord we pray.
Start with nine. Add eleven, then subtract the starting five.

Meanwhile, in the backyard, a series of commands ending with
the verb, to be, works its way to the seminar to be born. So
there aren't enough revolutions to keep the faculties of ten
universities busy on the talk shows more than six weeks, the
producer whined as he fingered his abacus, and all the tragedies
begin to look the same to children of forty, so I propose we
develop a show involving Martians, Laotians and Rosicrucians

perhaps in a co-ed dormitory at a school in the Midwest or,
anyway, someplace where beer is illegal before the age of con-
sent. With that, the German contingent left, as it does every
night, the format and crept stealthily toward the Common Mar-
ket (I have enough of these hyphens to last three hours and
from then on you and your eyes are on your own), humming a little
night music, the room filled with students who never took history.

SAVANT

The rain played out for him
in chords and the wind dances scales
around it. The laughter of the chil-
dren counterpointed to the melody.
The clear voice of the melody was his
mother. His father was percussion.

NO THANKS, I'M TRYING TO QUIT
(after Norman Mailer)

I've lost track of Patrick Benko
but I know he's not the id saying
a rosary of despair for his twin or
the ailing President who arranges death
for their father. Six days now, I've

worn sandals, still I can't find Grace.
Breakfast was spoiled by the huntsman
outside Salt Lake City. No one wanted
to be the guy who fired the blank.

Leading men die until it's a wrap, but
the kid in the heart suit gets in the
last word. Chicken 'n Biscuits: he always
hated those half-ass mountain diners anyhow.

THE ASCENSION OF GORDIE BRICE

When I was thirteen I was George Kell and I
played third base for the Detroit Tigers and
took a full swing at a pitch from Bob Feller
on my front porch and I hit Gordie Brice in
the side of the head. He had been sitting in
front of where I was standing and stood when
he shouldn't and his brother Al and I both
thought I had killed him, the crack was so
loud, but he never even fell down. Instead, he
jumped from the porch to the ground and called
for us to hold him down, he was flying and he
couldn't get back if we let him go. We sat him
back down until he spoke normally again, then
went up the alley to their house where their
grandmother was baking and she gave us warm bread
and butter and we never spoke of this again.

THE ELECT

Interviewer: How long have you been here?

Translator: Five days.

Have you had anything to eat in those five days?

Translator: No.

Interviewer: And has the baby had anything to eat?

Translator: No, nothing.

Days without mornings, trying to work in a dark room;
the mothers of the dying fix the hair of their young;
the children hold out empty hands as the photographer
walks away. We see the pictures after our dinners and
as usual, ask the gray voices of witnesses to,
"Please lighten up a little, we can't, for Christ's sake,
have a steady diet of meals without kittens or cake."

And so, elected to look ahead, we create the finer arts
of dance and dinner, we invent the tie that costs more
than an egg; the gown made of meat, the shoes of bread
and slap down the corridors of the House For The Dying
in our loose slippers, clown suit and nose, a senator's
handshake and, for the children, those flat rag dolls.

The train of our leaving holds exactly so many hundred,
tickets bought in advance, the passengers know who they are
and the others are not invited: the sordid, the dark
or the dying; only the healthy are allowed in heaven,
only those with coats are invited to sit here at the fire.

Or else is it as if we have learned that Jesus had no more
to say, that his uncle the red rabbi held his own table
groaning past midnight, that the gods of all our temples
are more comfortable over here, by the elegant windows?

It is as if we have heard that, our banquet over, we can
go now, we can make soup of gold, bread of velvet, and leave
the stones behind for those who must learn how to drink them.

THE LAST RESORT

Summer is over, they're putting the umbrellas away.
The tables are rolled into the big room inside by
the hall and the menus are changed to the warm foods.
In a few weeks the waiters will be fewer and older
and the waitresses will be called that or "Girl" again.
On the street outside the traffic will be going some
place when a week ago they were looking for a place
and old men will be sitting indoors, looking at youth
on glass screens in darkened rooms, their losses feeling
distant and less clear. There will be no sun at their
backs and strangers will tell them afternoon has ended.
And on the street, the tables and umbrellas are gone.

THE PRESIDENT'S NEW CABINET

Oh yes, you can tell by his eyes
that he's wearing a mask, that he can play
the scales with both hands, that they're
still trying to fix his father's watch.
You can see the dishes weren't done,
the Buick won't start, the letter home,
ripped open, still lies on the kitchen floor
(the wrong address!) and his lip won't heal
unless he learns to eat beef without choking.

That was the afternoon of the dance, the holiday
they told all of our names in the headlines,
the week of the wrong taxi home, the night
we purchased, literally, a false eye
and worried about the swearing-in bible, those

members guilty of tomorrow, well-dressed,
not a coffin in a carload, a Pentacostal answer
to foreign, each one the apple of his mother's

solid credentials, when you're crowding about,
always on time for a meal no, we're sorry, tall, hard
in our hopes and incapable of stuttering in English.

BUT THE BUSINESS SCHOOLS ARE FILLED
WITH HAPPY CHILDREN!

I woke up this morning and nothing changed:
I am still an old man. I need a blanket and a
pair of bedsocks to sleep these night and my
favorite song was written before my children had
been born. And they have children of their own.
There are other cliches about my age, but I've
grown sick of hearing them. Still, I do miss the
birds the young will never hear outside their
windows and the taste of whiskey after lunch. But
I am grateful that I have less time to suffer the
voices of politicians promising a better world ahead.
And the men of God who praise him for their wealth.

AM/PM

He woke that morning with a gripping
pain in his belly, a pain without
politics or hunger that made his
abdomen stiff as an expensive drum
that made him wonder if he'd begin
his day with loud, echoing fart
or on a stretcher being hurried
bellowing with pain to a white van
trimmed in red and flashing lights.

When he got downstairs though, he was
greeted by the sound of rushing
water and a somewhat frightened daughter
with a shower handle in her hand and
when he found the off switch to the
pump and the number for his plumber
his best dog's nose was flowing blood
from the stray cat's paranoia and
when he had staunched the poor dog's

wound with ice, a deputy with a paint
sample asked to see his car and hear where
he had been before the dawn and he fixed

that. And it wasn't until evening and
he felt his belly tighten that his eyes
flew open and he thought of his mortality again.

THE RUINS

The shadow of an erased portrait
crosses an old man's face as he answers

another man, once the boy who asks this
question of another man, still older.

This is the dust of a warm sun vanishing at
noon years before. Other years, waking

from a dream forgotten, he watched faces
he'd remembered fading as his eyes opened. He

is a mother's greatest sorrow, a portrait
erasing itself in its vanishing light.

IN ANOTHER DREAM I WENT BACK

to my old school and nobody
knew me. My teachers had all died,
which is probably true in this world
as well, but the kids were still

there unchanged but they didn't know
me but it was time for the lunch
so I took my old place at the long
cafeteria table and wondered if I should

start condemning the food as I did
in the past but as I write about this
the new cat, a ten-week-old kitten,
leaps up on my bed and bats at my pen

which skids over the page, stopping my
brain for awhile. Until now, having played
her 'till voices on the beach below me
jerked away her attention and I stumble

back to this page, I no longer can think
of anything interesting having to do
with missing friends or dead teachers
and the cat's back so we're going to lunch.

WORK SHIRT

The dog barks steadily in the room below
me. It is Sunday, September fifth, twenty
twenty-one, the day before Labor Day, and
he thinks the guests leaving their car in
the lot out back have come to see him. I don't
know if the President is visiting Detroit
tomorrow, but I do know if the dead can turn
over in their graves, Marx is a small, polished
marble by now. My father has been dead forty-
eight years in two months. I still have his
rosary in a drawer back home, and my wife
threw out remnants of his last blue shirt
I wore this summer, too far gone to lie still
on my shoulders. Today I'll call my sister
who is dying. Her husband is a banker, but I
love her without guilt. I'm sure our father
did as well. There are two subjects we will
not discuss though: one is death, of course,
the other is this blue shirt I won't wear.

SEPTEMBER

About a half a mile out, the gulls are
diving, feeding on the small fish that
come near the surface for warmth.
A few weeks ago, warm water sent them
up for cooler air. Up here on shore,
yesterday's dog is barking again today,
calling ours outside to play. I wake
from a morning nap and feel the season's
first cramping in my legs: time to
sleep with closed windows and the smell
of burning oil in our rooms; when it was
wood, its burning air made these places
more comforting, but aging lungs have
put an end to that. The clear air while I
can still bring it in brings a quicker
fall into deep sleep and dreams move more
rapidly, but this pain wakes me quicker
than before and small fish rise to
their fates as they always have, while
strange dogs go on barking at my door.

SEPTEMBER SONG

I

We are at a place between music and a river,
dressed in a new wool, in reds, browns, in gold
woven to be unnoticed, in the colors of cock
pheasants preening for the gunmen, or large
deer, their booming racks blind to wooden bows.

On my desk, the realistic statue of a bull
lowers his head at the wall, ceramic muscle
pulsing along his legs, his back. No swordsman
waits; on his spine is a plug. For two weeks
I removed it to pour whiskey into a glass.

II

Friday.
The clouds discuss snow.
We come to a wood,
to a clearing in a wood
or to some other impasse
we call comfort.

Under the sky
nothing moves,
under the earth,
less.

If
I turn to you now
in this new cold
it must be
as something more than
a blanket, as
something warmer
we are not familiar with.

III

This flies die between the two windows,
their noise like thoughts escaping in a classroom
while a spectral teacher instructs death
by hanging. I have forgotten how many nights
before it is October now, how many bits of sky
and water will stutter from blue into gray.
Already the children cough in their beds, already
the engines in their chests are slowing to a wheeze.

Listen. There is a sickness that comes here each year
and it has come on time again, a visiting priest
no one thought to cook the meats for, a gaunt man
at the door in your castoff shirt; Listen:
I talk to you every year about this and over
the same glass; this year's let's order champagne.

MINDSCAPE: HIS 83RD SUMMER

Ten years ago a doctor treated me for cancer
and I advised her on the training of her Husky pup.
I didn't charge her, but insurance paid for me
so in a way, I guess we came out even-steven, unless
her puppy's dead and I guess I'm not. For some reason
I think of this because, when I woke up from my
nap this morning, a lady bug was crawling up my window
screen. It might have been the one I wrote of weeks
ago, or it might not; at any rate I wondered for
a minute if this might be an omen of some kind. I
warned her of her burning home last time and she ig-
nored me. This could also be the reason for the bites
on both my ankles that I got while I was sleeping
which, while not supernatural, bother me much more
than these idiot thoughts that help me come awake.

LOSSES

There was another in this house last night.
We were too early counting up the earlier ones
to notice it. That happened during the last
half dozen or more, since memory becomes our way
of denying guilt. It's all so boring anyway;
every time we run the water 'till it's warm enough
we kill our children in the future, every day we
roll through life, we crush a dream. To live is
murder every morning, ask the ocean or the sky
we think we came from and return to when we die.
A nation mourns, a city weeps, the years go by.

TALKING LATE AT NIGHT TO THE YOUNG

Quoting inexactly from the book you can't find,
you work your way lie by lie through the 20th century.
The children, as usual, are carefully inattentive:
the sinking of the Maine not your fault and you lack blame
for the invention of the macaroni or the movie star; it
was an even older sibling who went panting to the Coliseum
and the Ramadan Motel, who helped pay for the guitar string.

Sunday a father will offer you his decade, a mother
will praise the future of your own wayward child.
Someday looking up or down at the surgeon's knife, you'll
wish for a lie of your own, invent your own life support
marked, DAWN, or tell it to remain as it is; someday
you will lie here like me: wrapped in the night's stiff blanket
counting all the words adding up, finally, to yourselves.

LABOR WITH THE SACRED

Yes and there goes Grandad off to work in the American morning
with his two sons, a bologna sandwich in one hand, the throat
of a colleague in the other, the soldier, the realtor, and the
advertising man; by car, bus or subway and an oink, oink here
and an oink, oink there, here a boss, there a boss, everywhere a
boss, boss, and where do they put my right arm when my right arm
isn't wanted? and who are all these tightened faces, giving out
"hard answers to difficult questions," these simple little masters
of complexity, smiling for the trustee who polishes off the chair
but never has to sit in it and why must I go off every morning
like an ulcer's grand uncle who sits, cup in hand, palms damp,
before the Critical Reasoning Committee? Why do the rich man and
the poor man's son dine out each day, the only items on the menu?

MARGARINE

Chatting by the fireside, the cognac properly warmed
we can quietly watch the century slide off unnoticed
except for its thirty or forty million gaping scars
and the way the sleeping cat flops its tail and, perhaps
opens one tiny eye as a shadow passes her warm corner.

When I was a boy, I remember, the gas jet in the stair-
well could still be opened, the lamp fixture on the ban-
nister still hissing, ignorant of the wiring and the
switches that we'd had on our walls all this time, and
my cousin could frighten my mother when he turned it on.

Later, when his ship went down in the North Atlantic,
he was saved, but not with his sniper's rifle or the
small carved piece of ivory he had taken for me in some
port bar, American military scrip accepted. He did, how-
ever, get a fine Italian dress sword and Libyan dagger.

And later, wounded in his second war, was robbed of his
Russian gun and scope in the hospital in Tokyo, more
interested, anyway, in the tiny Japanese actress who
visited his bedside every day. Remember Abbot and Costello?
Remember the early Dean Martin, Jerry Lewis, remember

Rocky Marciano valiantly making white men feel better
or the small button, orange in color, with which our
mother made the pale grease in the bowl look butter
yellow, the first ersatz from a conquered nation, its
cells congealing within our own, its hatred so like ours?

Or the anger of the men on Sunday afternoon, their beer
bottles and glasses of whiskey clashing against each other
on the kitchen table, blue shirt sleeves rolled up and
smoke filling the room slowly, with their increasing voices
and each one of their bitter, unpredicted deaths

bringing us now to our own, filling this empty room with
the sound now of my voice, of yours against the hollow of
time, the valley we find no rest in; against our daily
need we accept the first tiny click of the capsule, the
staining of the substance in the bowl, the fingers yellow.

SEPTEMBER 11, 2021

The clear sky and the clouds are near
enough in color to be the horizon, vanishing
in the smoke of a fire far away. Downstairs
the Irish bagpipes broadcast loss remembered
by many and still suffered by a few. To a
man just sworn to Congress, these are days to
claim an unearned glory; to a widow growing old
they're nights to feel the summer growing cold.

CRESCENDO

Down the beach a small dog is barking with
the insistence of Chinese water torture; soon
our shepard will join in, then the hound next door
as I give up and come awake, a dinner I thought
I was eating vanishing from the table I had
fashioned in my sleep. Then, as I listen farther,
waves crash in and simmer underneath the cracking
voices of seagulls and crows in combat for
the rotting sturgeon on the sand below and, as
I wake more, I wish both sides luck, hoping
one or both will carry off the stench that is
arriving at my consciousness just now. A screen door
opens; another closes; a voice calls to a voice
that laughs; this is all happening. There; there is more.

DAVE KELLY has published 16 books and chapbooks of poetry and experimental prose. He has received awards from the National Endowment for the Arts, the New York Foundation for the Arts, and the Poetry Society of America. His mother loved him but didn't like him very much. His father played catch with him in the backyard and taught him to box. Dave has degrees from Michigan State University and from the University of Iowa. He retired in 2009 from the State University of New York at Geneseo, where he was Poet-In-Residence and a professor of English. He now lives on a modest pension with his wife, Sylvia, on his dandelion farm in upstate New York and the family cottage on Lake Michigan.